Freaky Fish

Lynn Huggins-Cooper

Copyright © QED Publishing 2008

First published in the United States by
QEB Publishing, Inc.
3 Wrigley, Suite A
Irvine, CA 92618

This edition published by
Teacher Created Resources, Inc.
6421 Industry Way
Westminster, CA 92683

www.teachercreated.com

Library of Congress Control Number: 2008011765

ISBN 978-1-4206-8649-4

Author: Lynn Huggins-Cooper
Edited, designed, and picture researched by:
  Starry Dog Books Ltd.
Consultant: Sally Morgan

Printed in China

Picture credits
Key: t = top, b = bottom, l = left, r = right, c = center,
FC = front cover, BC = back cover.

A = Alamy, C = Corbis, D = Dreamstime.com, F = Fotolibra,
G = Getty Images, HB = Hippocampus Bildarchiv,
IQM = Imagequest marine, ISP = iStockphoto.com,
P = Photolibrary, PS = Photoshot, S = Shutterstock.com,
SDB = Starry Dog Books, SPL = Science Photo Library.

1 C/ © Hal Beral; 2–3 ISP/ © Tammy Peluso; 3br ISP/ ©
Chuck Babbitt; 4t S/ © Fukuoka Irina, 4b ISP/ © Chuck Bab-
bitt; 5 ISP/ © Harald Bolten; 6t C/ © Bruce Robison, 6b C/
© Bruce Robison; 7 A/Visual&Written SL © Mark Conlin/
VWPICS; 8t ISP/ © Susan Stewart, 8b SPL/ © Fred McCon-
naughey; 9 D/ © Watermark1; 10b G/ © Norbert Wu;
10–11 G/ © Norbert Wu; 11t IQM/ © Peter Herring; 12bl
© Dominique Weis, UBC, Kilo-Moana cruise, University of
Hawaii; 12–13 P/ © Oxford Scientific; 13b P/ © Richard Her-
rmann; 14b P/ © Doug Allan; 14–15 National Oceanic and
Atmospheric Administration; 15 G/ © Norbert Wu; 16t P/ ©
Max Gibbs, 16b G/ © Norbert Wu; 17 G/ © Norbert Wu; 18t
HB/ © Juergen Schraml, 18b C/ © Hal Beral; 19 D/ Dzain; 20t
G/ © Gary Bell, 20b P/ © Fredrik Ehrenstrom; 21 ISP/ © Dan
Schmitt; 22t G/ © Norbert Wu, 22b SPL/ © Tom Mchugh; 23
P/ © Karen Gowlett-Holmes; 24t PS/ © LUTRA/NHPA, 24b
S/ © J. Helgason; 25 D/ © Anthonyjhall; 26t SPL/ © Christian
Darkin, 26b G/ © Chris Newbert; 27 G/ © Peter David; 28bl
D/ © Tritooth, 28–29 SDB/ Nick Leggett.

Contents

Cool fish

Freaky fish are found everywhere, from the depths of the oceans to muddy riverbeds. At least 28,000 **species** of fish are known to exist, and new species are being discovered every year.

▲ *Many fish are now protected.* **Aquarium** *fish are bred in captivity rather than being caught in the wild.*

▼ *The great white shark has a terrible reputation for being a* **man-eater**, *and has been over-hunted because of this.*

Endangered

In 2007, the World Conservation Union described 1,201 species of fish as being threatened with **extinction**. Their list included species such as the Atlantic cod and the great white shark. Fish are at risk because too many are taken from the oceans by fishermen, their habitats are being destroyed by pollution, and too many tropical fish are being caught to be sold as pets.

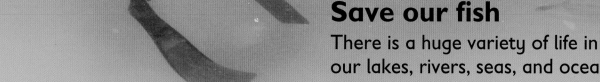

▲ *The whale shark is the world's largest species of fish. It can be up to 50 feet (14 meters) long, which is longer than an average school bus.*

Save our fish

There is a huge variety of life in our lakes, rivers, seas, and oceans. Some deep-sea fish produce strange points of light. Some fish are cleverly **camouflaged**, some are extremely poisonous, and there is even a vicious vampire fish that sucks the blood of other living fish. The world is full of freaky fish, and they are all worth protecting.

Terrors of the deep

The ocean depths are home to some very strange fish. Some have terrifying teeth. Others have small, light-producing cells on their bodies, which attract **prey**.

▲ At night, marine hatchetfish rise to a depth of 164 feet below the surface to feed. They return to deeper water before dawn.

Marine hatchetfish

Marine hatchetfish live at depths of 650 to 19,680 feet (200 to 6,000 meters) in the Atlantic, Pacific, and Indian oceans. Small cells, called **photophores**, on the undersides of their bodies, give off tiny spots of light that point downward. These lights may attract mates. They may also lure prey from below.

Spookfish

Some types of spookfish are also known as barreleyes because they have tube-shaped eyes. Barreleyes live deep in the Atlantic, Pacific, and Indian oceans, at depths of 1,310 to 8,200 feet (400 to 2,500 meters). Their sensitive eyes point upward and are able to detect **predators** swimming in the dim water above them.

◀ The bones of a barreleye's skull are so thin that you can see its brain between its eyes.

The barbeled dragonfish is a fierce predator in spite of its small size—about 6 inches (15 centimeters) long.

Barbeled dragonfish

Barbeled dragonfish live in **tropical** oceans at depths of up to 4,920 feet (1,500 meters). The female has a long **barbel** under its lower jaw that it waves backward and forward to attract prey. The barbel has a light-producing **organ** at the tip, and the fish can flash the light on and off. As soon as prey draws near, the dragonfish snaps it up.

Amazing facts!

The young of some dragonfish have eyes on the end of long stalks, unlike their parents.

Clever tricks

Some fish perform amazing tricks to keep themselves safe from predators and to catch their prey.

Porcupine pufferfish

The porcupine pufferfish eats small creatures and shellfish that it finds on the ocean floor. Feelers hanging down from its nostrils help it to find food, such as crabs, shellfish, and sea urchins. When it finds its prey, it crushes it in its beak-like mouth.

▲ *The royal gramma lives among the coral reefs of the Caribbean Sea, around the Bahamas and as far north as Florida.*

Royal gramma

The royal gramma, also called the fairy basslet, is half purple and half yellow. Its attractive colors make it a popular aquarium fish. The most unusual thing about this fish is that all the young are born as females. The females can change to become males if there are not enough males around.

◄ *When the porcupine pufferfish is alarmed, it **inflates** itself by swallowing water. Its spines, which usually lie flat, stick out. This helps it to scare away predators.*

▶The male Siamese fighting fish looks after his bubble nest. If any eggs fall out of the nest, he spits them back.

Siamese fighting fish

Siamese fighting fish are found in **rice paddies**, ponds, and streams in Thailand, Indonesia, Malaysia, Vietnam, and China. As the female lays her eggs, the male fish catches them in his mouth and spits them into a nest of bubbles that he has made.

Amazing facts!

A male Siamese fighting fish is aggressive toward other males, and will even attack its own reflection in a mirror.

Peculiar predators

Fish have some strange habits when it comes to catching food. Some eat fish bigger than themselves. Others slash at their prey with a sword!

Swordfish

The swordfish is named after its long, sharp bill, which looks like a sword and is at least one-third of the fish's length. The fish can grow up to 15 feet (4.5 meters) long. Feeding mostly at night, it uses its snout to slash at prey. The swordfish rises to the surface looking for fish, such as mackerel, bluefish, silver hake, butterfish, and herring, as well as squid.

Oarfish

There are four species of oarfish, or ribbonfish, one of which is the longest **bony fish** in the sea. It can grow to an incredible 51 feet (15.5 meters) long—about the width of a basketball court. Oarfish live in the deep ocean and have rarely been seen alive. Occasionally they wash ashore, giving rise to stories about sea serpents.

▲ *Oarfish have no teeth. They sieve small creatures through **gill rakers** in their mouths.*

Black swallower

The black swallower is a light-producing fish that lives up to 4,920 feet (1,500 meters) below the surface in tropical and **subtropical** waters. It has the amazing ability to stretch its stomach up to three times its size when it eats, so that it can eat fish bigger than itself.

▲ *The black swallower opens its mouth wide to eat fish whole and then slowly digests the food.*

▼ *The swordfish uses its bill to defend itself from predators, such as the shortfin mako shark. Very few predators are fast enough to catch a speeding swordfish.*

Amazing facts!

Swordfish have been known to push their swords through the sides of small fishing boats.

Weird and wonderful

Some fish look as though they have come straight from the pages of a comic. One looks like a stilt walker, another has a mouth like a cartoon duck, and one is shaped like a guitar!

Tripod fish

The tripod fish lives at the bottom of the **equatorial** oceans. It stands on its three long fins and waits for tiny **crustaceans** to bump into the fins near its head. Then the fish grasps its prey with these fins and directs the prey into its mouth.

◀ The tripod fish only grows up to 14.5 inches (37 centimeters) long, but its three long fins may extend to nearly 3 feet (1 meter) long!

Snipe eels

Snipe eels can be as long as 5 feet (1.5 meters). Their two jaws bend away from each other at the tips, and their teeth hook backward. This helps them to catch shrimps. Snipe eels prefer to swim in open water rather than near the bottom or the surface.

▲ *Snipe eels swim with their mouths open, and catch the long antennae of passing shrimps on the hooked teeth on their jaws.*

Shovelnose guitarfish

The shovelnose guitarfish was living before the time of dinosaurs. It lives in the **Gulf of California**, and is shaped roughly like a guitar. The shovelnose guitarfish eats crustaceans, such as crabs and shrimps, that it finds on the seabed. It has lots of small, round teeth that look a little like rocks.

▶ *The shovelnose guitarfish prefers to live in shallow water. Buried in the sandy seabed, it can be difficult to spot.*

Fish in the freezer

Even in very cold water, fish can survive. The freezing waters of the Southern Ocean are home to at least 270 species of fish. The fish that live there need to be specially adapted so they do not freeze solid in the extremely cold temperatures.

Blackfin icefish

The blackfin icefish has a type of natural **antifreeze** in its blood, which prevents ice crystals from forming in its body. This helps it to survive in sub-zero temperatures. It has no red blood cells, so its blood carries less oxygen than most fish. To make up for this, it has a large heart that beats twice as fast as other fish. It lives in the Southern Ocean and southern Atlantic Ocean.

▼ *The blackfin icefish spends most of its time resting at the bottom of the sea. They do not move very much due to the cold.*

Snailfish

Snailfish live in both cold and warm waters, at shallow depths, and as deep as 24,600 feet (7,500 meters). One-third of their body weight is a jellylike substance made mostly of water. This makes the fish more buoyant, or able to keep afloat.

▲ *Snailfish have pink and gray, jellylike bodies. They look like giant tadpoles in shape.*

Amazing facts!

Some Antarctic fish can die of heatstroke if the temperature rises above a chilly 42.8 °F (6 °C).

Bald notothen

The bald notothen is another fish that has a special **protein** in its blood that stops it from freezing in the cold waters of the Antarctic. This fish lives underneath the ice shelf, where it eats tiny krill and larvae.

▲ *To keep themselves safe from predators, newly hatched bald notothen swim up into the ice that lies several feet below the surface.*

Vicious vampires

Vampires are not only found in creepy castles at Halloween! Some fish also suck blood from living creatures, and others have extremely scary teeth.

▼ *The candirú's body is almost see-through, making it hard to spot as it swims in the Amazon River.*

▼ *A viperfish is seen here chasing a small prey fish. Viperfish hunt at night in fairly shallow water, luring prey with their photophores. They return to much deeper water by day.*

Candirú

The candirú is a tiny freshwater fish that lives in the Amazon River. To find its prey, it tastes the water to detect a water stream coming from the **gills** of another fish. It follows the stream and slips inside the fish's gills. Spines around the candirú's head dig into the prey fish and hold the candirú in place so that it can feed on the fish's blood.

Viperfish

Viperfish are among the fiercest predators of the deep. A viperfish's sharp, fanglike teeth are so long that they do not fit inside its mouth, but curve back close to the fish's eyes. The viperfish uses its teeth to stab its victims. It swims at them with great speed and spikes them.

Common fangtooth

The common fangtooth is a really scary-looking, deep-sea fish. It gets its name from the sharp fangs that stick out of its enormous mouth. Despite its fearsome appearance, it mainly eats tiny **zooplankton**, as well as any other creatures that float or get sucked into its gaping mouth.

▶ *When the common fangtooth shuts its mouth, the two long teeth on the bottom jaw slip into two tubes on either side of the fish's brain.*

Amazing facts!

The common fangtooth is so ugly that its nickname is "ogrefish"!

Hard to spot

Fish have some very clever disguises. They can be so well camouflaged that they are virtually impossible to spot. Some look like lumps of stone, others look like pieces of seaweed.

▼ *The devil scorpionfish looks as if it has weed or **algae** growing on it. Its skin changes color slightly to blend with its surroundings.*

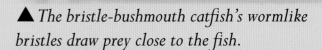

▲ *The bristle-bushmouth catfish's wormlike bristles draw prey close to the fish.*

Ancistrus ranunculus
Bristle-bushmouth catfish

The bristle-bushmouth catfish lives in the rivers of South America. It has long, bristly tentacles on its snout, which it uses to find food. This has led to it being called the Medusa Head. In Greek mythology, Medusa was a monstrous woman who had snakes for hair. She could turn people into stone.

Devil scorpionfish

The devil scorpionfish is a master of disguise. It looks like a rock or chunk of dead coral. The fish has **venomous** spines on its back and fins that it can raise to defend itself. The poison can be fatal to humans.

A male leafy sea dragon's tail turns bright yellow when he is ready to mate.

Leafy sea dragon

The leafy sea dragon is a close relative of sea horses. It lives in the warm oceans around Australia. As with sea horses, the females lay the eggs, but the males carry them in a pouch until they hatch.

▶ *The leafy shapes on the sea dragon help it to hide among floating seaweed or **kelp** beds.*

Poisonous parts

Many fish and other water creatures are poisonous. Most of them only use their poison in self-defense and not for attack.

Weevers

Weevers have poisonous spines on their gills and on their first dorsal fin (dorsal fins are on a fish's back). During the day, weevers bury themselves in the sand on the seabed, leaving just their eyes poking out. As shrimps and small fish swim past, the weevers snap them up.

▲ *The blue-ringed octopus is only the size of a golf ball, but it is one of the world's most poisonous animals.*

Blue-ringed octopuses

The blue-ringed octopus is a mollusk, not a fish. Blue-ringed octopuses live in tide pools in the Pacific Ocean, from Australia to Japan. A blue-ringed octopus will camouflage itself as it hunts for crabs and shrimps. If attacked by a predator, it turns bright yellow with blue rings, and bites the attacker. Its poison is created by bacteria in the octopus's **salivary glands**. A single octopus carries enough poison to kill 26 adults.

◄ *The weever's poison is for defense. If a person stood on the fish, the fish's spines would sink into their foot. This would release a poison that causes a great deal of pain—worse than a wasp sting.*

▼ *The stonefish is the most venomous fish in the world. It can be very difficult to spot among the reef's rocks.*

Stonefish

The stonefish lives on coral reefs in the shallow, tropical waters of the Indian and Pacific Oceans. Its mottled colors provide good camouflage among the rocks. The stonefish eats shrimps, small fish, and crustaceans. The dorsal fin on its back is covered in many venomous spines. The poison can be fatal to humans.

Amazing facts!

Poison from the stonefish causes very severe pain to people who touch them.

Slimy fish

Fish produce slime from their skin. The slime protects them from parasites and diseases, and helps them to move through the water. It can also make them taste bad, as well as make them harder to catch.

▼ *To get rid of its own slime, the hagfish ties itself in a knot and sweeps the knot toward its head to scrape itself clean.*

▶ *At night, some types of parrotfish secrete a mucus cocoon around themselves to mask their scent from predators.*

Parrotfish

Parrotfish are named after their ridged, parrot-like beak, which they use to scrape algae from coral reefs. The slimy cocoon that they sleep in at night provides good protection from parasites, which suffocate in the slime.

Hagfish

If another fish tries to eat a hagfish, the predator gets a mouthful of slime. When threatened, hagfish ooze out a small amount of thick, white fluid. The fluid absorbs seawater and swells to form a thick, heavy slime. The slime suffocates predators by clogging their gills.

Slimeheads

Slimeheads are commonly known as roughies. They live in the cold, deep waters on the eastern and western edges of the Pacific, the eastern Atlantic, and the seas around Australia and New Zealand. They breed later in life and live longer than most fish, up to 150 years!

▼ *Slimeheads, such as this southern roughy, have a network of slime-filled dents in their head.*

Tricky travels

Some fish make incredibly long journeys. They may swim for more than 1,864 miles (3,000 kilometers)—three times the length of the UK. Some fish actually walk on land using their fins as legs!

▲ *Young European eels are called glass eels. After they have entered* **fresh water**, *they are called* **elvers**.

Salmon

Salmon hatch in small streams. After a year, they swim to the ocean, where they live for several years. They then make an extraordinary journey back to the stream where they hatched to **spawn**.

European eel

The European eel begins life in the Sargasso Sea, in the North Atlantic. It then swims to Europe or North Africa. Females travel inland along streams and rivers, and live in fresh water for 7 to 15 years. They then return to the Sargasso Sea to lay their eggs and die.

◀ *Scientists believe that salmon use the sun, moon, and stars to find their way across thousands of miles of ocean.*

Mudskippers

Mudskippers can breathe through their skin long enough for them to skip across a muddy area of shore. They can even survive for days out of water as long as they keep their gills wet. Special storage bags behind the eyes hold seawater, which is used to keep the **gill flaps** damp.

▼ *Out of water, a mudskipper uses its fins as legs to push itself along.*

Amazing facts!

If a mudskipper dries out, its gills begin to stick together and it cannot breathe.

Funky fishing

Some fish have developed unusual ways to catch their prey. They "go fishing," using a fake fish on the end of a line that is attached to their head.

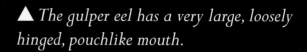

▲ *The gulper eel has a very large, loosely hinged, pouchlike mouth.*

Gulper eel

The gulper eel is also known as the umbrellamouth gulper or pelican eel. Its large mouth allows it to swallow fish much larger than itself. It also has a special organ on the end of its tail, which lights up. Scientists think this may help the eel to attract prey.

Warty frogfish

Warty frogfish have a long spine under their mouth, at the end of which is a lure that looks like a small fish. The lure is used to draw prey into close range, so the warty frogfish can snap it up. Warty frogfish are well camouflaged. They can change color until they match the surrounding sponges or corals.

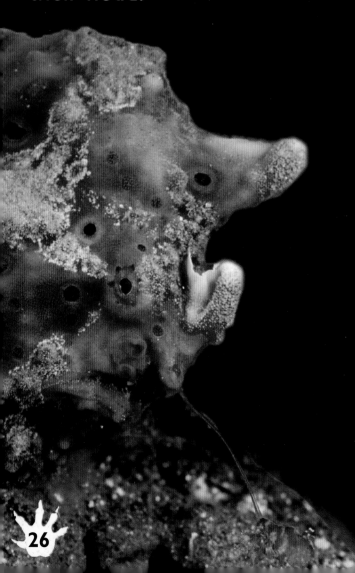

◄ *A warty frogfish waves its lure in the hope of attracting a prey fish to swim close by.*

▶ *Special light-producing bacteria live inside the lure of the fanfin anglerfish.*

Anglerfish

Anglerfish have a huge mouth and lots of sharp teeth. On the front of their head, they have a long spine with a fleshy lure at the end. Prey see the fleshy lump wriggling and think it is a worm to eat. The jaws of the anglerfish snap shut automatically when a creature touches the **bait**.

Amazing facts!

The stomach of an anglerfish is able to stretch to twice its normal size to hold large prey.

Make it!

Make a **shoal** of your own freaky fish to hang from the ceiling or to swim across the wall of your bedroom.

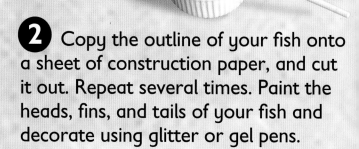

> ✂ *You will need:*
>
> Construction paper
> Scissors
> Glitter
> Gel pens
>
> Aluminum foil
> Glue
> Hole punch
> Ribbon or string

1 On the Internet, do an "images" search for "fish" to find lots of pictures of different fish. Choose your favorite fish, or pick a fish from the pages of this book.

2 Copy the outline of your fish onto a sheet of construction paper, and cut it out. Repeat several times. Paint the heads, fins, and tails of your fish and decorate using glitter or gel pens.

28

3 From a sheet of aluminum foil, cut out lots of rows of scales.

4 Put some glue along the straight edge of a row of scales. Starting at the tail end of one of your fish, stick the row of scales to the fish's body. Repeat, overlapping each row, until the body is covered.

5 To hang your fish from the ceiling, punch a hole in the top of each one, and attach some ribbon or string. You might want to make a shark, too, for added excitement!

Glossary

algae

Certain types of plant that grow in or near water. Algae do not have ordinary leaves or roots.

antennae

Long feelers on the heads of creatures such as insects and crustaceans.

antifreeze

A liquid that lowers the temperature at which water freezes.

aquarium

A glass container in which fish and other water creatures and plants are kept. It can also be a type of zoo that you can visit to see many different types of fish and other water creatures in tanks and pools.

bait

The food used to lure creatures so that they may be caught. Fishermen attach bait, such as maggots, to a hook on the end of their line.

barbel

A whisker found on the heads of some fish. Barbels are used as feelers. Some fish use them to find prey.

bony fish

A bony fish has a skeleton made of bone. Most fish are bony fish, but some fish, such as sharks, have skeletons made completely of stretchy cartilage.

camouflage

To disguise in order to hide or conceal. A fish that is camouflaged is difficult to spot because its patterns or colors blend with the background rocks, reef, or seabed.

crustacean

A type of animal that has a hard outer shell. They live in water, such as crabs, shrimps, or lobsters, or on land, such as wood lice.

elver

A young eel.

equatorial

An equatorial region is on or near the equator. The equator is the imaginary line that goes around Earth at an equal distance from the North and South poles.

extinction

A destroying or dying out. When the last of a species has died out, it is said to be extinct: no more individuals exist.

fresh water

Water that is found in ponds, streams, lakes, and rivers. Unlike sea water, fresh water is not salty.

gill flap

When a fish breathes, it takes water in through its mouth. The water passes through the gills, which remove the oxygen from the water. The water is pumped out again through the gill flaps.

gill rakers

Bony, finger-like sticks found in the gills of some fish. The gill rakers help to support the gills.

gills

The gills of a fish are the parts of its body that extract oxygen from water, allowing the fish to breathe. They are usually found behind the head of a fish.

30

Gulf of California

Part of the Pacific Ocean between the coast of Mexico and the peninsula of Lower California.

inflate

To get larger, usually by filling with air or gas. A balloon inflates when you blow into it.

kelp

A thick, rubbery type of seaweed that grows quickly. It forms underwater forests in shallow oceans.

man-eater

A large creature that kills a person in an unprovoked attack is described as a man-eater. Sharks and tigers, for example, can become man-eaters.

mollusk

An animal with a soft body and no supporting bones. Most mollusks, such as snails, have a hard shell to support their body, instead of bones.

organ

A part of the body, such as the heart or liver, that does a special job.

photophores

Light-producing organs found in some deep-sea fish. They produce light in the murky depths of the ocean. The light can act as camouflage for the fish. It may also attract other fish of the same species, or prey.

predator

A creature that hunts and kills other animals for food.

prey

An animal that is hunted and killed for food by another animal.

protein

A food group needed for growth and the repair of injuries. In some fish, it helps prevent them from freezing.

rice paddies

Flooded fields used for growing rice.

salivary glands

Salivary glands are found in the mouth. They make saliva, which is the liquid that we call spit.

shoal

A large group of fish, usually of the same type, that swim together.

spawn

The eggs of fish or other water creatures, such as frogs. To spawn is to lay eggs.

species

A group of animals that share characteristics. Animals of the same species can breed with each other.

subtropical

The regions next to the tropics are called subtropical.

tropical

Tropical relates to the tropics—the area on either side of the equator. The tropics are usually hot and damp.

venomous

A venomous creature uses poison to paralyze or kill its prey.

zooplankton

Animal plankton, made up of small crustaceans and fish larvae.

Index